The
BEAR
Who Lived
at the
PLAZA

The BEAR

Who Lived *at the* PLAZA

Ward Morehouse III

Published by BearManor Media
2015

Published in the USA by:
BearManor Media
PO Box 1129
Duncan, Oklahoma 73534-1129
www.bearmanormedia.com

Printed in the United States of America
Cover and book design by Bob Antler, Antler Designworks

For my wife, Katherine Boynton

with my love,

Ward

And for Will, my son

with love,

Dad

Preface

This appeared in the first edition of Plaza Magazine.

Anna, my Hungarian nanny, speaking into the gilt and ivory phone by the front desk of The Plaza Hotel asked for "Mr. Morehouse, please." Age five, I was by her side in a blue serge suit with short pants.

"Hello!" boomed a voice with a distinctive Southern accent, on the other end of the phone. It belonged to Ward Morehouse, Savannah-born drama critic and columnist for *The New York World-Telegram and Sun*, and for many years a Plaza resident. He was also my father and, although my parents were divorced, I was making one of my countless weekend trips to visit him in the huge castle on Central Park which I learned later was the most famous hotel in the world.

"It's Anna—and Wardie, Mr. Morehouse," Anna said. "Hi ya, Anna! Come on up!" he said. My father and stepmother, Rebecca Morehouse, a *Time* correspondent, lived in Suite 660-661, which was a large (enormous, it seemed to me then) one-bedroom suite with a small kitchen and, for a short while, believe it or not, a real live bear the size of a small Scotty.

Today, my father had a special treat. He went into the bedroom and asked me to wait in the living room. Two minutes later he growled, "Come in!" I gingerly opened the door and he leaped out of bed in his blue serge suit wearing a wolf mask and growling. I turned heel and ran for it, ecstatically laughing.

Animals, real and imagined, were very much a part of my father's life at The Plaza. He once brought me a lion cub from Johannesburg, South Africa, we called "Joburg," and my mother, a former Broadway actress, talked about being given a (real) white fox when she lived there. Then there was the aforementioned bear, which he bought from the Boon Vanit Company in Bangkok, Thailand, for $35. Soon the bear went to live on a farm in Georgia and eventually had a long life with the Ringling Bros. Circus.

On a typical Saturday, my father still had some work to do, so to keep me busy he encouraged me to order room service. I loved soup in the gleaming silver bowls and the sandwiches and chips and Coke that Anna also got me sometimes. His "work" was interviewing stars appearing on Broadway for his column called "Broadway After Dark," which I later adopted as the name of my own theater column.

My father interviewed a steady stream of stars at The Plaza, including a glamorous, dark-haired young lady named Audrey Hepburn, talking about her show *Gigi* at Broadway's Fulton Theatre. "Oh, I thought I was such a blooming flop on the opening night, but then, at the end, the audience was wonderful. Jolly wonderful!" she told him. Others he interviewed were Ginger Rogers, Robert Mitchum, who was in a new movie, not a play, and Rosalind Russell, who was staying at the Pierre Hotel across Fifth Avenue. And while waiting for my father, Anna sometimes took me to the small barbershop to get a haircut. It was on the mezzanine above where the new Champagne Bar is today.

I'd run back to 660-661, Anna trailing behind in the wide corridors and crying, "Wardie, wait for me!" Then we'd head over to Broadway to see a new play or musical. Often, we didn't stay for the entire show but only a half hour or so before moving on to the next one. In those days, my father, who knew all the theater "house managers," got permission to take me in during the middle of a show, and if there wasn't a seat to be had, they'd find a chair to put in the aisle temporarily.

Later as a journalist and author, I interviewed the late Hildegard Neff, who was also known as "the incomparable Hildegard" or just Hildegard. She told me of singing in The Plaza's famed Persian Room for then U.S. Senator John F. Kennedy when she slipped and fell near his table. "You see, Senator, I've fallen for you!" she said as she composed herself.

Like millions of people around the world, I, too, have fallen for The Plaza, the most lavish, the most spectacular, and the most legendary hotel almost since the day it first opened its doors in October of 1907.

Contents

Ward Morehouse III, aged three and a half down by the East River
(WARD MOREHOUSE III COLLECTION)

Introduction

The characters in this curious book—some of who not coincidentally also happen to populate my curious family—include a bear named Bangkok who for a time lived at The Plaza Hotel; one of New York's most famous theater columnists and drama critics who had a lifelong passion for plays, travel and beautiful women, as well as wild animals; a beautiful Broadway actress who went on to publish the *Theater Information Bulletin* for half a century; one of the first woman producers on Broadway, who discovered Cary Grant and ran the City Center for Music and Drama; and my father's widow (and my stepmother) who had an illustrious journalism career all her own (she interviewed Cary Grant four times).

One piece of advice my father gave me on his deathbed has never left me: "Never give up." Hence this book, and many others.

One of the very first Broadway shows I ever saw starred Jean Arthur as Peter Pan and Boris Karloff as Captain Hook in a 1950 Leonard Bernstein musical adaptation of J.M. Barrie's *Peter Pan*. I spent most of the show hiding behind the theater seat in front of me because of Karloff's rather fearsome (at least to me at the time) Captain Hook. Another early show I saw was Mary Chase's *Mrs. McThing* starring Helen Hayes. Chase had won a Pulitzer Prize for Drama for her play *Harvey*, the movie of which starred Jimmy Stewart. *Mrs. McThing* was a sort of "morality play" that kids shouldn't grow up too fast. The theater has, in one way or another, kept me from doing just that!

My book, *Broadway After Dark: A Father and Son Cover 100 Years of Broadway*, is a lively and colorful portrait of some of the greats and near-greats of the New York theater. The father in this literary partnership is Ward Morehouse (1895-1966), the legendary Broadway critic whose "Broadway After Dark" column ran for decades in *The New York Sun*. His interviews with Eugene O'Neill, William Gillette, Laurette Taylor, Gloria Swanson and many others transport readers to golden eras of Broadway. I picked up where my father left off, writing my own "Broadway After Dark" column, as well as reviewing plays for Reuters, the *New York Post*, *The Christian Science Monitor*, *Black Tie Magazine* and BroadwayAfterDark.org. I was a columnist for Reuters for several years in the early 1990s. My interviews with Neil Simon, Joan Rivers, the late Wendy Wasserstein and Hugh Jackman help to bring the book into the 21st century. A poignant link between the past and the present is supplied by Katharine Hepburn, who talked with my father in the 1930s and 1940s for *The New York Sun* and with me for Reuters and the *New York Post* in the 1990s and 2000.

My father joked he wanted "Room Service, Please" on his tombstone. I've written eleven books on hotels altogether including *London's Grand Hotels* and my most recent book, *Millennium Biltmore: A Grand Hotel Born of Hollywood Dreams*.

> *"So we beat on, boats against the current,*
> *borne back ceaselessly into the past."*
> —(F. Scott Fitzgerald, *The Great Gatsby*)

The
BEAR
Who Lived
at the
PLAZA

1

Gentleman of the Press

Late in 1924, after working on the *Savannah Press* and *Atlanta Journal*, my father got into the *New York Tribune*'s dramatic department. He inaugurated his "Broadway After Dark" column after joining what became his 'signature' paper, *The New York Sun*, which rivaled the *Herald Tribune* as New York's premier afternoon daily newspaper. While working at the *Savannah Press* he moved from his parents' home into Savannah's historic DeSoto Hotel and began his lifetime love affair with living in hotels.

He put some of his own early newspaper experiences into his first Broadway play, *Gentlemen of the Press*, finished in December of 1927. It was also a movie starring Walter Huston. "We went into rehearsal in July and hoped to get to tour ahead of the competitive newspaper play, *The Front Page*, written by Ben Hecht and Charles MacArthur and produced by Jed Harris," my father said.

Harris, however, brought in his play [to New York] *in mid-August. "Gentlemen of the Press" played a week in Atlantic City prior to New York and opened at the Henry Miller* [the Stephen Sondheim Theatre] *on what must have been the hottest night of the year. Critic Heywood*

Ward Morehouse interviewing husband-and-wife acting greats Alfred Lunt and Lynn Fontanne

Broun paid tribute to the true atmosphere, the characters, and the dialogue, but said the story wasn't as strong as that of "The Front Page."

In January of 1929, with talking pictures experiencing their nervous beginnings, Paramount began shooting "Gentlemen of the Press" at the Kaufman Astoria Studios.

Walter Huston was spotted in George M. Cohan's [and Ring Lardner's] baseball play, "Elmer the Great," and given his first screen job—the role of Wick Snell. With the shooting nearly ready to start, it was discussed that there was no actress for the role of Myra, siren of the play.

So we all went immediately to Tony's and there, in the haze of that famous back room with celebrities, of sorts, piling over the bare tables, we found ravishing Kay Francis; she was resting comfortably behind a Tom Collins. She was tall, dark, and interesting looking but had

Ward Morehouse signing his biography of George M. Cohan for James Cagney who won an Oscar portraying Cohan in Yankee Doodle Dandy

Ward Morehouse in his office at the old New York Sun Building at 280 Broadway

Clark Gable, who had known my father since the 1920s.

made far more appearances in Tony's than she had on the Broadway stage. But the day of just 'looking it' [in silent movies] was gone forever. Could she act and how was her voice? She was hustled over to Astoria; in the first test her voice came through, clear and vibrant. Her screen career began that very day.

Besides *Gentlemen of the Press* my father did what he called "an emergency rewrite job" on a play called *Forsaking All Others*, a vehicle for Tallulah Bankhead, later made into an early talkie. And there was his 1937 Broadway play, *Miss Quis*, starring Peggy Wood, about a small-town spinster who inherits a whole town.

2

Bangkok, the Bear

One of the most intriguing stars of this book is a bear called Bangkok, who stopped briefly at San Francisco's Fairmont Hotel on the way to my father's apartment at The Plaza Hotel in New York. In one sense, Bangkok was symbolic of my father's love of the unpredictable, in drama and life. Bell boys and even an assistant manager mistakenly ran for cover. Bangkok was totally untrained and unmindful of commands. In my father's own words is a story called "My Pet Bear" which originally appeared in *Cosmopolitan Magazine*. "I own a bear…I got him in the mysterious and irresistible city of Bangkok, Thailand, while flying eastward and homeward from an around-the-world spin last spring," he wrote.

I paused in colorful Bangkok, crossed the muddy Choa Phraya River, and spent an afternoon in the sales yard of the Boon Vanit Company, Ltd., merchants of jungle animals, on Burapa Road. I got the cash-and-carry prices on a baby elephant ($400), a baby tiger ($400), and a black panther ($350) but it was a playful Himalayan bear cub at $35 that caught my fancy, and I left the outdoor menagerie with the cub in tow. He was about the size of a full-grown Scotty, six weeks old and fed on goat's milk.

I carried my pet to Bangkok's Hotel Oriental and later, with considerable difficulty, and with the help of wide-eyed airline attendants, got him to New York via the airways, not as regular air freight, but along with me in the planes on which I rode, making hectic stopovers in Hong Kong, Tokyo, Honolulu and San Francisco. In San Francisco he made a wreck of the bathroom in the elegant Hotel Fairmont. He did likewise in my apartment at The Plaza Hotel in New York.

I then took him by car to the 700-acre Franklin farm in Bulloch County, Georgia, near the tiny village of Register, and introduced Bangkok, as I was now calling the cub, to my somewhat alarmed brother-in-law H. V. Franklin, Jr. He mumbled something, glanced at the health certificate I had brought all the way from Thailand, and told a farm hand to run and get some milk— cow's milk. That was in May of 1952.

Well, during a recent holiday from my job as a theater columnist-critic for New York's World-Telegram and Sun, I returned to H. V. Franklin's acreage and found that my little Thailand cub had changed startlingly. He is about ten months old and weighs around 125 pounds—I was told in Thailand that he will get to weigh 400. His home is in an elaborate pen built around a tall sycamore tree. Bangkok has become king of the Georgia farm and pet of the village of Register, to which he is frequently taken on a leash.

Bangkok has also become a tireless actor; the larger his audience, the better his show. He is never savage unless molested during a meal; try to take an ear of corn or a chicken wing from him and his growl is that of an animal of the jungle. But it is a gentle treatment that he gets from the Franklins, loving attention along with the best food any bear ever had. He will eat and drink anything but his appetite is enormous. No goat's milk since he left the Orient, but every day he has plenty of milk from fine cows and six pounds of dog food in three regular meals. He also gets, in generous handouts, Southern fried chicken, soda pop, potatoes and tomatoes, biscuits and bread and coconut cake, peanuts and oranges and catfish. He will stand on his hind legs for candy, grapes and lump sugar.

Bangkok is allowed out of his pen frequently, but never without being watched. He's had one fight with the Franklin's bird dog and a kitten. Beauty, the saddle horse, is quite terrified of him and stays well out of his reach. I was told out in faraway Thailand by the animal man, one Luang Visal Bochanakich, that Bangkok would probably like candy of all kinds, and I saw evidence of it in Georgia when we got him to the big crossroads store of Moses Jackson Bowen. He ate a large assortment of penny candies, in many shapes and colors, but when he reached Main Street in the village of Register, he was still hungry and gobbled up a pint of ice cream in the H. H. Olliff drugstore.

Farmers of Bulloch County drop by, ostensibly to talk to my brother-in-law of cotton, wheat, corn and soybeans and of the spring planting, but they always turn their gaze toward Bangkok's pen and ask, "How's that bear getting along?" Such a question had just been put to "H", as my wife's brother is called, at a filling station on Route 301 one afternoon when a Franklin farm hand drove up and rushed toward him, greatly agitated. "The bear's gone, the bear's gone!" he cried. "Got out of his pen and we can't find him—we've looked everywhere."

"Why," "H" said, "you couldn't run that bear off the farm."

He got into the car with the man and they drove to the house and made a tour of the nearby woods, looked into the barn and the cowshed, and the tool shed and the kennel and finally entered the house, via the back door.

There, upon the kitchen table, sat Bangkok, with a sugar bowl in his paws. He looked up unconcernedly and then went along with his licking of the bowl.

"H", in his Georgia drawl, observed quietly, "That bear is more fun than anything else this farm ever had —and we'd like to keep him...but someday we might sell him to a circus or a carnival or something. Either that, or let my Broadway brother-in-law keep him in his New York apartment. We've heard tell that Mr. Morehouse likes to bring 'em back alive."

Bangkok was indeed lively at The Plaza, nipping the maids' feet, gobbling up any morsels left from room service. My late stepmother, Rebecca "Becky" Morehouse, whose late brother H. V. Franklin ran that farm, had a less rosy story to tell about Bangkok's life at The Plaza. Shortly before she died in 2013 I asked her if Bangkok ever got up on their bed. "Heaven's no! That would have been the end!" she laughed. Becky, a fine journalist in her own right, had more gentle guests in their suite. She interviewed Cary Grant four times. The rowdiest Grant got was taking off his shoes after a hard day filming *North by Northwest*. With his stockinged feet on the coffee table, he at first was difficult during this interview, refusing to talk about the movie or anything else he was working on. Filming had been frantic and he was stressed. Becky steered the conversation to an easier topic to warm him up, asking him how he enjoyed his stays at The Plaza. He related that on a previous visit he had

Cary Grant PHOTO BY GLYNN LEWIS

run down to The Plaza kitchen to ball out the chef for serving only two halves of English muffin instead of three as was done in London. That changed the picture. Grant was roused out of his funk, and he and Becky completed the interview.

Ironically, for all the time I spent with my father at The Plaza, I didn't run into Bangkok there, or in Georgia. I did, however, have another member of the wild animal kingdom who lived with me for a while at a nearby hotel. My father brought "Joburg," a lion cub, to me when my mother and I lived at the Hotel Seymour which used to house the famous Coffee House frequented by George Gershwin. Joburg was the size of a medium-sized cat. Unfortunately, Joburg only lived a few weeks in the comparatively cold climate of a New York City hotel room. Later, I would write extensively about the menagerie of animals that lived in other New York hotels, including a baby alligator at the Waldorf-Astoria. That hotel's carpenters constructed a wooden ramp to make it easier for the alligator to slip and slide into a bathtub. Salvador Dali kept a cheetah at the St. Regis Hotel. When the manager complained to Dali that he would have to replace a Persian rug his cheetah had destroyed, a bellhop was seen carrying a Dali painting to the manager's suite.

Bangkok wasn't around, fortunately, when my father and I played "Wolf." My father would get into bed, fully clothed in his signature blue suit, don a rubber wolf's mask and call, "Come in!" I opened the door gingerly and he leaped up growling and I turned heel and ran for it, screaming.

Some days we would light gunpowder in the kitchen sink. He opened a shotgun shell and poured the black powder into the sink and "POOF!" and there I'd go, yelling again. Years later, my son Will and I played handball with a rolled-up pair of socks on the night The Plaza threw a press party for my book, *The Plaza Hotel: An Intimate Portrait of the Ultimate Hotel,* in the second floor Vanderbilt Suite overlooking Central Park. That was shortly after September 11, 2001, when the entire world was focused on the "9/11" terrorist attack on the World Trade Center. Besides my son and my former wife, Elizabeth Morehouse, my mother, who had lived at the hotel with my father early in their marriage, attended with my stepfather Roderic Rahe.

3

George M. Cohan

In 1942 my father's book, *George M. Cohan: Prince of the American Theater,* burst upon the literary scene. I say 'literary' because it was more than a theatrical biography. It captured an American phenomenon with his faults as well as triumphs. As a boy of four or five, I enjoyed leafing through the pages of this book long before I knew who George M. Cohan was. It made Cohan, too, feel like a member of my family. Unbeknownst to me as a boy, I would write a book on the Hudson Theatre, *Discovering the Hudson,* where Cohan had his greatest success in the 1920s. In the book, my father recalls a meeting with Cohan in the dead of winter when the 'Yankee Doodle Dandy' was in a reflective mood.

"I accepted his invitation to lunch and went immediately to 993 Fifth Avenue," my father wrote. At the time Cohan was playing President Franklin Roosevelt in *I'd Rather Be Right* on Broadway.

> *There I found Cohan in better spirits than I had at any other time during the years I knew him. He was gay, chipper, and most garrulous. With coat collar turned up, hat down over his eyes, and his hands thrust into the pockets of his light topcoat, he headed for the Central*

SELWYN THEATRE

PARK SQUARE, BOSTON
SELWYN & CO., PROPRIETORS AND MANAGERS
FRED E. WRIGHT, RESIDENT MANAGER

Week Beginning Monday, Dec. 3, 1923
Matinees Wednesday and Saturday

GEORGE M. COHAN

In His New American Dramatic Comedy, in Four Scenes

"The Song and Dance Man"

Written by Mr. Cohan

ABOVE: *George M. Cohan*
show program
RIGHT: *Portrait of George M.*
Cohan
(WARD MOREHOUSE COLLECTION)

Park reservoir track, only two hundred yards or so from
his front door. Soft, powdery snow filled the January air.

"Here we go. Gee, kid, I've been going around this
lake for more than twenty-five years. I know every tree.
Why, when I first started I was watching Matty pitch for
the Giants and Jack Johnson was the heavy-weight champ
and there was a fellow named Taft in the White House. I
met Taft, but I've never met Roosevelt, even though I am
doubling for him in 'I'd Rather Be Right.'

"Say, just look at that Fifth Avenue skyline. When I

first started out here, those high buildings weren't there —only residences…Nothing better than this, kid. Lot of my friends play golf—I don't…My routine these days is to come out here in the afternoon, give a show at night, and be around at The Plaza for a bit around midnight."

We were coming into the home stretch around the reservoir, moving along briskly now. Cohan looked at me and grinned.

"Can you make it, kid?…Good for the legs. I need it, too. Until the show came along I hadn't danced in about ten years. I got to keep in shape all of the time; I'm getting on, you know…Got another birthday coming along soon and perhaps had better begin lying about my age. But you guys'd never let me get away with it, will you?"

We finished our walk and, as usual, went back to relax in front of Cohan's fireplace.

4

Eugene O'Neill

Eugene O'Neill, generally never one to go out of his way for newspaper men, must have been in a good mood when he wrote my father at London's Savoy Hotel to extend him a visit at his castle in the Tours section of France. O'Neill wrote in a letter dated March 29, 1930:

Le Plessis
Saint-Antoine du Rocher
(Indre-et-Loire)
March 29th, 1930

Dear Ward Morehouse:

Sure thing! I'll be glad to see you. Arrange to come down and stay overnight with us. There's a good train from Paris to Tours around two or two-thirty p.m. that gets in Tours around six. Wire me a couple of days ahead so I'll be certain to be here and say what day you're coming and I'll meet you at the Tours station. This place is ten kilometers out in the country. You can get back to Paris comfortably by the next evening if you're in a hurry and still have a night and a morning here. I warn you, I've got nothing much to offer in the way of news since I don't want to declare myself much in advance as to the nature of the work I'm doing. [It was <u>Mourning Becomes Electra</u>.] I'm certain you'll like it here. I can promise you a grand lungful of Touraine country air and a spell of peaceful repose—and you can give me the New York news!

All kind regards,
Eugene O'Neill

O'Neill was then 41. He and Mrs. O'Neill (Carlotta Monterey) had presumably happy years in the Touraine. They kept house—thirty-five rooms of house—at Château du Plessis, removed by a hundred miles and more from the whirl of Paris. My father picks up the story from there:

That evening at Château du Plessis, we sat before an open fire in the large high-ceiling living room. Eugene O'Neill talked freely until well past midnight of his self and his writings. His speech was always thoughtful, it was never hurried.

"If I had an idea," he said, "that I'd have to repeat myself, that I had to stand still, I'd quit writing plays. I'd call it a day. I write primarily for myself, because it is a pleasure, and it would cease to be that if I started repeating. I could have gone on forever with plays like 'Anna Christie,' or with the expressionism of 'The Hairy Ape,' but I'm interested in trying to do better things."

"Now, this new play of mine is the hardest thing I've ever tried. God knows, it's the most ambitious. I've done

the first draft. I'll do a second, then lay that aside and start on something else. Later I'll come back to it, and perhaps I may have something. I don't want to talk of its content. That hurt me with 'Dynamo.' I just want to finish it, call a stenographer from Paris, and then mail it to the Guild. I've been at work on it for a year. Carlotta seems to think it's all right." ("Wonderful," was the word Mrs. O'Neill used to me.)

The dramatist-son of a grand old actor sipped his Coca-Cola and sat gazing at the burning wood chunks. "You see," he said, "I've found out something. I've found out that I ought to take more time. Looking back to 'Dynamo,' I did eighteen long plays in eleven years. That's too much. If I could go back I'd destroy some of these plays, say, four of them—'Gold,' 'The First Man,' 'The Fountain,' and 'Welded.' I've written, I think, forty plays—twenty long and twenty short. In my notebook I have ideas for thirty plays, perhaps thirty-two. That's work for a lifetime."

"Would you," I asked, "destroy 'Dynamo'?"

"No, but I'd rewrite it. 'Dynamo' had in it the makings of a fine play, but I did it too fast. And it was silly of me to mention a trilogy. And I wasn't surprised that they jumped me about it—that was but natural after 'Strange Interlude.'"

He paused. "The play of mine," he said, "for which I have the greatest affection is 'The Great God Brown.' Next, 'The Hairy Ape' and then 'Strange Interlude.' My favorite short play is 'Moon of the Caribbees.' I think the best writing I've done for the theatre was in 'Lazarus Laughed.'"

"I've been remarkably lucky, I think, in the matter of actors. Certainly the performance of Walter Huston in

'Desire Under the Elms' was tremendous. Exactly what I had in mind. And there were splendid performances by Paul Robeson in 'The Emperor Jones' and by Lynn Fontanne in 'Strange Interlude.'"

We rode the next day in his Bugatti racer and got it up to 106 kilometers an hour. We swam in his concrete pool and wandered over his forty acres, with his Gordon setter and Dalmatians coming along. Never one for chatter, Eugene O'Neill, but on this beautiful morning in the Touraine he talked rather constantly.

"I love it here," he said simply. "But I've never had any idea of living here permanently. No nonsense about renouncing America. There's such a thing as being sensible patriotic. But living away from America has been a good way to get to know America—to see things you couldn't see before."

And so I found Eugene O'Neill when he lived in France. They told me good-bye as the chauffeur whirled through the driveway in Mrs. O'Neill's magnificent French car. He had on a heavy sweater and she was trim and in smart Parisian sport clothes. He extended his hand and grinned. "Tell them we're coming back," he said. "We're coming to live in New York or Georgia or California or somewhere."

I was in the big car. The engine roared. The car shot forward and I was off for the Tours train, which was to take me back to the boulevards and the bewilderments of Paris.

5

Jeanne Eagels and *Rain*

M y father's own favorite play wasn't O'Neill's *Strange Interlude* or *The Iceman Cometh*. It was *Rain,* based on the W. Somerset Maugham story, *Miss Thompson.*

"Rain" came into the Maxine Elliot Theatre on a November evening in 1922, and the opening brought forth an emotional demonstration never exceeded in the theatre of this country and century. First-nighters stood and screamed when the curtain fell upon Sadie's denunciation of Davidson at the close of the second act; they were as wild as spectators at a football game.

I occupied a seat in the rear of the balcony on that opening night and experienced one of the most genuinely stirring moments in all my theatre-going years in the final scene of the third act when Sadie's long-silent phonograph broke into the haunting strains of "Wabash Blues," her gesture of complete disgust with all mankind. She had learned only too bitterly that the Reverend Mr. Davidson, the foe of all evil, who had finally convinced her that she must return to San Francisco and repent her sins, was an idol with feet of clay. Jeanne Eagels had her greatest night and she was acclaimed, and so was the play, the next day by the enthusiastic critics—Hammond, Broun, Mantle and Woollcott. Miss Eagels achieved a stardom that had been honestly earned and she went on to play the role of Sadie for 174 weeks.

For a time, in her all-too-tragically-brief Broadway years, the great actress took up residence in a floor of a brownstone on East 58th Street where my father was living in between hotels, just east of Fifth Avenue. Remarkably, this and another brownstone beside it are still there, left standing amid the avalanche and cacophony of post World War II skyscraper sprawl.

Eagels had asked my father if she also could get a place in his building "to get away from the crowds"…"and soon she arrived at those modest quarters with a cook, maid, chauffeur and there were times, I believe, when a butler put in an appearance!" he wrote.

"Before the coming of the erstwhile Sadie Thompson, life above the ground floor Mes Amis restaurant had never been particularly serene, but now, once she had moved in, there was a forever bustle on the stairway…" he continued.

At the height of her fame, Jeanne Eagels penned some of her own story in the old *Theater Magazine.* "My father used to tell me not to tell my life story. He said people never told the truth about themselves," she wrote. "The temptation to romance is too great to be missed. My father was right. That temptation to romance stirs me now. But I will conquer it. In the first place I will give my right name. It is Joanne," Eagels said.

I am of crossed strains. My father was a Spaniard. My mother was from Dublin. They lived in Boston and I was born there. My father was an architect and not very successful. We moved to Kansas City. He designed some buildings there, but I don't know what they were. My

earliest recollection is of quarreling with some children
in our street who made fun of us because we used the
broad "a" in "bath" and in "laugh". My sister gave up the
contest. She consented to flatten her "a". I refused. I said
I would not be bullied into using a sound that was not
right. I loved combat. I love it now.

My debut on the stage was with an amateur organi-
zation of children. I was the gravedigger in "Hamlet" and
just seven years old when I made that debut. From that
time, with short intervals of school going, I played for
eight years. I played in a stock company in Kansas City;
I played in repertoire companies in the middle West; in
tent shows. I played all kind of parts—old women with-
out teeth …

Who cast a pretty girl for an old woman without
teeth? My husband. But we will forget him. Marriage I
have put behind me along with other unsuccessful ex-
periments.

W. Somerset Maugham, seeing the play which he had
prophesied might not be made from his published story *Miss
Thompson*, exclaimed at the performance of *Rain*, "I wrote the
story of the character from life and Miss Eagels has played it
from life. Where did she get that voice and laugh? She has convinced me there was a play in my story. No one else could con-
vince me. Not even those who dramatized it." Eagels continues:

I studied her, as I do every role, from the foundation
up. Some things we know but cannot put into words. I
knew how Sadie Thompson would talk and act and rea-
son. I knew that her voice must be hoarse, and harsh,
as though she smoked too many cigarettes or drank too
much whiskey. I studied her. It came to me that she was

Jeanne Eagels (WARD MOREHOUSE COLLECTION)

the best Christian of all the group in the play. I am sure of it. She had two Christian qualities, courage and honesty. The preacher was not, as many who see the play think, a hypocrite. He proved that by cutting his throat. He atoned for his sin. He was not a hypocrite but a fanatic. I sometimes wonder which are our real selves, the parts we play on the stage, or those we play off the stage? At any rate, I know the theatre has the most powerful lure in the world for me. It is stronger than love.

Jeanne Eagels appeared in an early "talkie," *The Letter*. Dave Kehr said in a July 2011 *New York Times* article that Eagels' "ability to seize and swim 'in the moment'—as generations of method actors would later characterize it—is formidably illustrated in the scene in which she shoots her lover, completely unconcerned with her appearance...a wild-eyed Eagels fires again and again, thrusting her gun forward with each shot..."

The more my father saw of her, the more she became the character she played in *Rain*. He wrote, "Theater-goers had stood up and cheered like spectators at a football game." Yet as the decade of the 1920s neared its end, the game was nearly over. She was depressed she never made it bigger in the movies.

"Her death came with shock in its suddenness," my father said. She had called at the Park Avenue Hospital in the late afternoon of October 3, 1929, and was waiting for a consultation with her personal physician when a convulsion seized her. Death was attributed by a city toxicologist to an overdose of chloral hydrate. The body, in a silver and bronze coffin, was sent for burial to her native Kansas City, which she had left in her teens to make her fame in New York.

"I was not at *The New York Sun* office when news of her death was received," my father continued. "But when I reached my typewriter the next morning, there was a memo rolled into it. It read: 'Please call Jeanne Eagels, 3:30 p.m.'"

6

Katharine Hepburn

Another famous resident of "midtown" Manhattan was for many, many years the late Kate Hepburn. I ended up interviewing her three times and did a number of other stories about her. She was always blunt, as when I asked her how she liked living in New York. She looked around the high-ceilinged living room of her brownstone and simply said, "I like it if you call this living in New York." I sat hanging on every word, dazzled I was with one of the biggest movie stars of the twentieth century. Amazed by her frankness and, at that time, beauty. Here's a story I did in the *New York Post* on her ninetieth birthday, after she'd finally moved out of Turtle Bay:

Old Saybrook, Conn.—One of Hollywood's last remaining living legends celebrates her 90th birthday tomorrow.

But there will be no fireworks, champagne toasts or star-studded parties for Katharine Hepburn.

Instead, one of cinema's greatest divas will spend a quiet day—virtually alone—in her isolated mansion on a peninsula that curls into windswept Long Island Sound at the mouth of the Connecticut River.

If it's warm, neighbors in her exclusive seaside community may see the four-time Oscar winner walk halt-

ingly on the arm of John Elmore, her driver of many years.

But Hepburn, who's in failing health, is more apt to be sitting before a roaring fire, gazing out at the light-house offshore and remembering brighter days.

That was when her seaside home in the tony Fenwick section was a veritable Hollywood East and her beloved "Spence" would stay here. In fact, Spencer Tracy's bath-robe still hangs in her bedroom closet.

"There's no celebration planned," Ellsworth Grant, Hepburn's brother-in-law, told the Post. *"She's too out of it. There's no reason to do it."*

Although a medical scare last year led her to move to Fenwick permanently—giving up the townhouse on East 49th Street in Manhattan that she bought in 1932—she has no serious health problems.

"She has the disease of old age," Grant said. "She walks a little, talks a little, but her memory is pretty much gone."

But her fans aren't willing to forget.

Old Saybrook will mark the occasion quietly tomor-row when First Selectman Laurence Reney visits Hep-burn with a bouquet of flowers from the town.

Also tomorrow, City Parks Commissioner Henry Stern will rename a half-acre garden in Dag Hammar-skjöld Plaza the "Katharine Hepburn Gardens."

And Sen. Joseph Lieberman of Connecticut has asked President Clinton to bestow the Presidential Medal of Freedom, the nation's highest civilian honor, on the great film star.

Lieberman's request is expected to be fulfilled.

Writer Henry Josten, a Hepburn pal, says that even if she were more up to it, "Kate" wouldn't want any fanfare.

Josten says, fifteen years ago, the actress objected to renaming the causeway that runs from Old Saybrook past her home the "Katharine Hepburn Causeway."

"If they do that, I'll never use it again and take the long way around to get home," Josten says Hepburn warned at the time.

Hepburn didn't turn away all local honors.

She once shelled out $10,000 for a fire engine the town needed—a deed repaid when the firemen named the vehicle "Old Kate."

Some said everything she did hinged on her mood.

"It all depended on what side of the bed she got up on," said Josten. "She could be the most charming person alive or bite your head off."

In luncheon interviews with her in 1994, she told me [this reporter] she had finally come to the point where she no longer minded being called a "living legend."

"I think it's all right to be called one now. I've been around a hell of a long time. I think I'm entitled to be called a legend, don't you? And I am living!"

And this is an interview my father did with her some decades earlier, in that same East Side brownstone where I, too, first interviewed her:

"I'm generally taken to be an intellectual," she said to me as she sat cross legged in the rear garden of her home in New York's Turtle Bay section. "But I do nothing but go on hunches. When I'm appearing in a play, all I do is to do the play—and rest and eat. I'm always so terrified on opening nights I wish I could be dead drunk through the first performance. I still think it would be a good idea to open plays with a matinee performance and then the

poor bloody actor would have less time in which to do a complete freeze. But that matinee idea is Ruth Gordon's —not mine."

"I've had seven or eight plays in New York. Those first nights, brother! They do get steadily worse. They're terrifying, they're horrifying, honestly. I'd like to own a theatre in Brooklyn and just never open on Broadway. I'll never forget the first night of 'The Philadelphia Story.' Dear Phil Barry protected me in that play—with the writing, I mean. And on the opening night the Lord came down and helped me get through. During the first performance of 'As You Like It' I felt much easier. In that play I could change things around—not the words, but the movement."

Miss Hepburn, now wearing an old white sweater, brown gabardine pants and old, thick-soled shoes, accepted the challenge offered by "As You Like It," which gave her her first Shakespearean role, and she was triumphant.

"I always wanted to play Rosalind and I always knew I was going to do it," she said. "I had a good time playing the part and I learned a lot. Somehow before trying that play, I'd often thought that the audiences were just sitting out there, waiting to lynch me, but Rosalind got me to believing that people had come to the theater to have a good time and that there was great friendliness out front."

Bonny Kate had a good time during the shooting of the film, "The African Queen" in the African wilds but she had an even better time in playing "As You Like It" in New York and on tour throughout America.

"When I was trying to learn to play Rosalind, I got to wondering to myself what the hell acting really is. I like

to act, but I also like to do many things—to clean a room, to walk, to ride my bike, to play tennis, to fiddle around in this garden. I don't like to do anything unless I really like to do it. Wouldn't have done 'As You Like It' without help from the wonderful Constance Collier [Miss Collier died in 1955]. She worked with me for about six months, every afternoon. Miss Collier was wise; she had a real zing and a zest for all that was good in life. She had a passionate belief in life and in people—and so have I."

7

Jean Dalrymple
and City Center

Jean Dalrymple, my father's second wife, was one of Broadway's first woman producers. In its obituary of her, the *New York Times* called her, "…a persuasive dreamer who brought theater to City Center," and then said of her, "…she abandoned a nascent acting career to become a successful publicist, then an even more successful manager of concert artists and finally a dynamic producer of music and plays for City Center and other stages…"

The *Times* continued, "Miss Dalrymple's stature in the New York theater world was enhanced by her uncanny ability to lure just the right actor for a particular role at a particular price that City Center, with its limited budget, could afford. Her skillful productions nourished and entertained audiences there from the 1940s through the '60s. Franchot Tone, a stage and movie star in the 1930s to 1950s whose work Miss Dalrymple always admired, thought of her as 'the tenderest little lady.'"

When she was writing vaudeville sketches, a tall, handsome, bow-legged young man auditioned for her and her partner. Her partner said he was all wrong. Jean said, "He's extraordinarily handsome and that's what we want." And that's how Cary Grant got his first speaking role on Broadway (even though it was a vaudeville sketch). Grant and she remained friends and some years later, when Grant became a spokesman for Faberge, he asked Jean to handle the public relations. He was that kind of grateful man.

But let's let her tell part of her story:

> *After producing my first play,* Hope for the Best, *I was accepted as an independent producer and for a while I became engulfed in scripts. So many came my way I had to engage to pay readers, although actually I consider this a great waste of time—theirs and mine. Unless a script comes personally from a well-known author or highly recommended by a play broker, it is almost always certain not to be worth the reading. Every producer will tell you that finding a hit among the batch of randomly submitted manuscripts is like finding a fine pearl in a restaurant oyster. Probably even rarer!"*

Jean was the instrumental, behind-the-scenes force in creating what became the City Center for Music and Drama. Regarding Mayor LaGuardia's proposed "Center of Performing Arts" for New York City at the old Mecca Temple, she wrote:

> *I told him I had read all about it in the newspapers and that I had been particularly interested in the project because during the past winter I had helped to present a series of concerts for the Treasury Department in that great barn of a place, Mecca Temple, which had been taken over by the city from the Shriners for nonpayment of taxes during the Depression. Local 802 of the Musicians' Union had furnished the orchestra, and I had pre-*

*vailed upon my gifted clients to appear gratis and we sold
the public Treasury stamps and bonds.*

*We gave six concerts, and José Iturbi, who was then
at the height of his popularity as a film star and is a concert artist, conducted the Tchaikovsky Pathetique No.
6 Symphony in B Minor and, for the second half of the
concert, played Tchaikovsky's great Concerto No. 1 in G
Minor, conducting the orchestra from the piano.*

*I always like to believe that it was these Treasury
Department concerts that convinced not only LaGuardia but also Newbold Morris that Mecca Temple should
be saved from the usual fate in store for this sort of old
building—to be razed and used as a parking lot.*

❧

For a few years, when I was a Broadway columnist for
the *New York Post* in the 1990s, I had an office in Jean's apartment at 150 West 55th Street across from City Center. The living room where I did my weekly column was complete with a
(non-working) marble fireplace. And best of all Jean was right
next door in the dining room or bedroom when I needed a
quote, which was often. Jean was on the board of the American Theatre Wing which she co-founded and that was, with
its Tony Awards, always in the news. Jean was literally just at
hand. She was as quick with her wallet as with a quote. I found
myself in debt by $1,500 for a reading of one of my plays at the
7 Stages Theatre in Atlanta once. After saying I was quite ready
to jump off the Brooklyn Bridge if I couldn't get the money,
she graciously wrote me—or 7 Stages—a check. While 7 Stages
agreeably waited for her check, I would several years later produce an "angel" for them who had deep and immediate pock-
ets. Stewart Lane put upwards of $50,000 into a late summer

run of the play I co-wrote with him, *If It Was Easy*. It won an American Theatre Critics Association nomination as Best New Play of the Year and opened in New York in the spring of 2001. Bruce Weber of the *New York Times* said, "You could count the laughs on one hand." I felt he treated the play unfairly since we had been rival columnists but couldn't prove it. In my father's day, critics sometimes sent others to review a play if they were prejudiced for or against a play's producer or writer. And yet when my father badly reviewed a play my godfather, Vinton Freedley, produced, they never spoke to each other again.

❦

Jean and my father were in Los Angeles for their honeymoon where they were working on writing a movie.

Jean wrote of this time:

… We had ten or twelve invitations for dinner and just as many for cocktail parties.

One of the invitations came from—I almost went into a Victorian swoon when I was introduced to him! —John Gilbert. I could not believe it when he singled me out and actually steered me to a corner of the room where we could sit and talk about—of all things—golf. Jimmy Cagney had told him I was a golfer and it seemed that this had become a veritable passion with John. We made a date to go out and play the very next morning and when Ward finally came to gather me up to go home, he found me still gabbing with John, flanked by Jimmy Cagney on one side and Cary Grant on the other.

He seemed almost annoyed by this and, bowing, said "Queen, if it suits your majesty, the chariot awaits." We all thought this very funny; even I did. When we finally were back in our bungalow—not late, as Hollywood parties broke up early in those days, and still do—we piled into our nice big double bed....

In those days Ward was very amusing and well organized. He usually got up about seven o'clock, went down to his office and pounded out his column. Sometimes he stayed at home and had what he called "a day of genius," during which he would call Noël Coward in London, Miriam Hopkins and three or four other stars on the West coast, order flowers sent by telegram to friends all over the world, and in other glamorous ways manage to spend a couple of thousand dollars. Ward once sent Dorothy Hall, for her opening in the Preston Sturges play, "Child of Manhattan," four hundred dollars' worth of orchids! When I took mild exception to this particular extravagance, he phoned down to the florist in the lobby of the Essex House and had them send up to me every single flower in the place.

"There," Ward said as they arrived by the bucketful, "that ought to satisfy you." And I had come home on the bus to save taxi fare! Of course I never let him know about this or my other economies as they only would have confirmed his opinion of me as a little girl who just never would catch on to big city ways. The fact that Miriam Hopkins always referred to me as "Little Joan"—she only started to call me Jean a few years ago—did not help matters any for me either.

Ward had, and has, the saving grace of humor, and virtually everything he did or said amused me. Some days I would come home from the office and find him entertaining not only, say, Tallulah Bankhead, Gertrude Lawrence and Leland Hayward but "a bevy of beauties," as Ward put it, unknown to me and even sometimes to Ward. This caused me considerable consternation only because it upset Pinkey, who had moved up from the Fifty-Third Street apartment and was now bartender at apartment 3802.

"Miss Jean," she would say, "that girl in the pink dress has two pairs of your stockings and a bottle of your perfume in her handbag." Or, "That pretty dark one over there took all of your lace handkerchiefs."

I would say, aghast, "You mean, stole them?"

She would sigh. "I don't think you can call it that because Mr. Ward told them to help themselves."

❧

Before Hollywood and Jean Dalrymple, my father said he almost quit the newspaper business to write plays full time. "I came closest in 1924 to quitting the newspaper game when an Army officer invited me to live, rent free, in the Statue of Liberty," he once wrote. "Yes, the Statue of Liberty. The officer was in command of a small Army garrison on Liberty Island. He invited me to live there so I could write in peace and quiet. One day I called in sick, packed up all my plays and ferried out to Liberty Island, intending to give up the then-enviable life of a newspaper reporter—9 am to 3 pm on one newspaper and then a double night shift!

"I climbed those 327 steps up to my new home in the torch …About ten that night I got up to gaze on all I'd left behind …lights from Broadway seemed to flicker on the water…the Hotsy-Totsy, Jack's and all the exciting news pouring out from those venerable establishments. …"

During WWII my father was a war correspondent— one of the only, if not the only, theater columnists ever to cover a war. In his own inimitable way his "war copy" was almost as colorful as that covering Broadway:

Sun Reporter Accompanies Largest Troop Shipment
Ward Morehouse Describes How U.S. Soldiers Eat, Sleep and Roll Dice with their Life Preservers On.

By Ward Morehouse, Special to the New York Sun, Copyright 1942, All Rights Reserved.

[Ward Morehouse, playwright, author and regular member of the staff of the New York Sun, who has described the United States at War in dispatches from camps throughout this country and the Caribbean area, now is with the American Troops somewhere in the European zone. The first article in a new series by Mr. Morehouse is printed in the New York Sun today and others will follow as they are received.] (Passed by U.S. Army Censor).

Aboard Troopship, Atlantic Crossing.
The blue-green and gale-swept Atlantic lies ahead in all its immensity. Cottony clouds fleck the sky and our troopship, carrying the greatest number of soldiers ever sent overseas in one shipment, zigzags onward and eastward.

From stern and from bow, from starboard and port, all you see is sea as our craft follows its carefully proscribed course, leaving a twisted trail of emerald foam in its wake.

A lean, sun-blackened, helmeted boy who hails from one of the clock towns of Connecticut is at his post on the submarine watch. A burly, thick-set sergeant, who used to operate a Ferris wheel with an itinerant Middle-West carnival, is on the alert beside his anti-aircraft gun. And a lank big-boned corporal, who was short order cook for a Niagara Falls hash house in his pre-army days, stands ready with the gun crew of one of the big ones.

The ship is jammed. Jammed! From bow to stern, from top to bottom, with bunks everywhere except in the funnels. Every bunk and bed is filled. Troops sleep on deck by day and by night—stripped to the waist, mouths open and life preservers within reach. No man moves a foot without it. A soldier's life preserver is something he takes with him to meals and to bed. I've already learned the trick of it and can tie a neat nautical bow and know that it will keep a man afloat, even a fat one, for thirty-six hours, once he's had to go over the side.

Two Meals a Day.
This is a war crossing in every sense. There's no need to tell you, Mr. Irving Berlin, who wrote This Is the Army, Mr Jones, *(no private rooms or telephones). Two meals are served daily—just two. Chow lines are forever surging up and down the stairways and through the corridors. One-way traffic frequently is enforced. Troops get their two meals in fourteen sittings, officers in four sittings. First call for breakfast for the men is 6:30 and feeding continues until noon; chow lines for dinner are formed before 3 and it's 8 or thereabout before the last man has had his loin pork chops, baked beans, boiled potatoes, apricots, bread and butter and coffee. A man may stand in line for an hour or more but he's not at the table for more than fifteen minutes.*

On this voyage, aboard this ship, I am living with troops who learned their stuff in the United States and who are now being rushed overseas to try it. Combat troops these boys are and they look it. Hard as rocks, and they show it. They've learned their war games on the varied terrain that the training areas of America afford – rolling country, rugged country, piney woods, sand hills, and treeless ground as flat as the floor. These young combat troops of America's new army are tough, eager, and helmeted and they're on their way. To me, whether they're regular army or drafted men, whether they're tall or short, lean or pudgy, all of them, here in the mid-Atlantic, have, definitely, that second-front look.

The Dominoes Gallop.
Aboard this eastbound and war-bound craft, over-laden with its great horde of physically fit humanity, the young men of this historic crossing are taking it as you might have known they would. They're eating and sleeping and working and wondering. They're griping and sweating and fretting and yelping. They're laughing and grinning and singing and talking and sprawling. They're crumpling greenbacks (dollar bills) as they flip out their greasy cards at stud poker; they're busy with dice, crouching on blankets on the decks, huddled together like quail in the broom sage, bending over and praying and changing to the rolling cubes.

They're reading too. Comic supplements, pulp magazines, detective stories, tattered copies of Yank. They're gazing and seldom is there a vacant spot at the rail. Crossing the Atlantic and making history, they're also seeing the Atlantic, now misty and wind-tossed, now soft and billowy and almost unwrinkled, now blue-black and now emerald-green, a sea that is as ever-changing in its colorings as in its patterns. To the great majority of these war-bound young Americans, this is their first crossing.

*And to many the ocean, their first ocean, is an all-day
show in itself.*

*A strange and exciting crossing this is. I've stood at
the rail and gazed seaward and tried to get the feeling of
voyages of other years. The ship is moving along power-
fully, serenely. The sky is clear and the sun is strong. You
are comfortable and well fed and certainly invigorated by
the salt air. The great expanse of ocean looks as it always
did. But upon your back there is a life preserver and you
weren't wearing it as you strolled the deck of the Beren-
garia or the George Washington or the Ile de France. And
if you glance to either side of you there is a boy in uni-
form at your elbow. The reverie is broken.*

Little Talk of War.

*It teaches you things, crossing the Atlantic by troop ship
—an armed camp afloat. I'm getting used to going from 9
am to 7 pm without a morsel and not minding—well, not
too much. I've seen more lieutenants than I ever thought
were alive. I've learned to climb into the upper bunk of a
double-decker without breaking an ankle or even sprain-
ing a leg and I've seen all the latest tattoo designs—girls,
snakes, flags, eagles, anchors—upon the chest and shoul-
ders of boys of this new army of ours.*

*I've talked to the officers as well as to the men, and
they are equally keen for the adventure that lies ahead,
but there is surprisingly little talk of war. A lieutenant
talked at length and interestingly, of the wilds of New
Caledonia. A captain told of his trip, as a civilian, far
into the vastness of Venezuela. A major went on raptur-
ously about the magnificence of Texas, where he teaches
school, practices law and runs a ranch, and with the ma-*

jor general, the only one aboard I had a session with on the state of the dram, past and present. To this general, this voyage serves as a return to the war. Two decades and four years ago he was wounded and decorated and now here he is again, on his way back—and again as a combatant.

So goes an Atlantic crossing, as of this very moment. Your ship is taking soldiers in unprecedented number to the war and to the front—to some front. The ship is alert from bow to stern; its guns are ready and so are its gun crews. It knows that an attack may come from either the sea or air—or both. It takes every precaution and no unnecessary chances, and no man moves step without his life preserver and that includes privates, corporals, and the general.

And this correspondent, too.

8

Joan Marlowe Rahe
and the
Theater Information Bulletin

Joan Marlowe Rahe, my mother, graduated from Stephens College where she studied with the great Maude Adams, who opened on Broadway in *Peter Pan* in 1905. My mother went on to co-edit and publish the *Theater Information Bulletin* for fifty years. It was a weekly update of plays on and coming to Broadway and Off-Broadway. Maude Adams, by the way, was one of my father's major conquests. I know what you're thinking. I mean as an interview subject. She repeatedly declined being interviewed. Success came over lunch at New York's old Colony Club, once located in the building that now houses the American Academy of Dramatic Arts. I include my mother's obit exactly as it appeared in *The New York Sun* as I couldn't have said it better.

Joan Marlowe, 88, Published Theater Bulletin
By Stephen Miller, Staff Reporter of the *Sun*, March 11, 2008

Joan Marlowe, who died Thursday at 88, was the co-pub-

lisher of the Theater Information Bulletin, *Broadway's version of an industrial newsletter.*

The Theater Information Bulletin *was a mimeographed weekly number filled with facts and figures about openings, closings, casts, credits, and attendance in the New York theater world.*

According to the self-appointed "Voice of Broadway," columnist Jack O'Brian, Marlowe and her partner, Betty Blake, knew more about theater than George Jean Nathan, Brooks Atkinson, John Golden, and Lee Schubert.

An aspiring actress herself, Marlowe dropped out of Cornell University at age 19 to pursue acting. She appeared in regional productions and in 1941 was on Broadway in a small role in Mr. and Mrs. North.

She had a future in theater, but not as an actor. Also in 1941, she married Ward Morehouse, then a drama critic and columnist for the old New York Sun.

She worked briefly at Newsweek *before reviving the* Theater Information Bulletin *in 1944 with Blake, also a* Newsweek *reporter. The publication had been a sideline for Sam Zolotow, a* New York Times *drama reporter. Marlowe and Blake invested their savings—$35, according to O'Brian—and went to work. The publication continued until the early 1990s.*

Marlowe's experiences pounding the pavement for acting jobs also became fodder for The Keys to Broadway *(1951), an instructional guide for fresh talent. It included suggestions for scraping by during fallow periods: babysitting, crocheting, greeting card artist.*

Marlowe and Blake also published New York Theater Critics' Reviews, *a reference work that was sold to* Playbill *in the early 1990s.*

She served as the president of the Outer Critics' Circle

CHARLES FROHMAN

—PRESENTS—

MISS MAUDE ADAMS

In a Play, in Five Acts,

PETER PAN

Or, THE BOY WHO WOULDN'T GROW UP

By

J. M. BARRIE,

PETER PAN	Miss MAUDE ADAMS
MR. DARLING	ERNEST LAWFORD
MRS. DARLING	GRACE HENDERSON
WENDY MOIRA ANGELA DARLING	MILDRED MORRIS
JOHN NAPOLEON DARLING	WALTER ROBINSON
MICHAEL NICOLAS DARLING	MARTHA McGRAW
NANA	CHARLES H. WESTON
TINKER BELL	JANE WREN

TOOTLES		VIOLET RAND
NIBS		LULA PECK
SLIGHTLY		FRANCIS SEDGWICK
CURLY	Members of Peter's Band.	MABEL KIPP
FIRST TWIN		KATHERINE KEPPELL
SECOND TWIN		ELLA GILROY
JAMES HOOK, the pirate captain		ERNEST LAWFORD

SMEE		THOMAS McGRATH
STARKEY		WALLACE JACKSON
COOKSON		WILLIAM HENDERSON
CECCO	Pirates.	PAUL THARP
MULLINS		THOMAS VALENTINE
JUKES		HARRY GWYNETTE
NOODLER		FREDERICK RAYMOND
GREAT BIG LITTLE PANTHER	Redskins.	LLOYD CARLETON
TIGER LILY		MARGARET GORDON
LIZA, author of the play		ANNA WHEATON

Redskins, Pirates, Crocodile, Ostrich, Lion, Pack of Wolves, etc.

Maude Adams the first actress in America to play the title role in J.M. Barrie's play "Peter Pan." MAUDE ADAMS PROGRAM *and New Drama Forum, an offshoot of the Drama Desk organization of reporters and columnists.*

Marlowe was raised in Ithaca, N.Y., the daughter of the city editor of the Ithaca Journal. Her mother had appeared in silent films.

A bon vivant who loved to dine with the theater crowd at Sardi's and 21, Marlowe was also known as a hard worker who insisted on getting each detail right. The story was told that she worked until midnight one Friday putting the final touches on an issue, and then gave birth the following morning.

JOAN MARLOWE RAHE

Marlowe was born January 7, 1920, in Ithaca, N.Y.; died March 6, 2003, in a nursing home in Darien, Conn.; married Ward Morehouse in 1941, divorced in 1948; remarried, to Roderic Warren Rahe, a chemist, in 1952; survived by her husband, her sons Roderic Warren Rahe, Jr., and Ward Morehouse III, an author who has written about theater for *The New York Sun*, and four grandchildren.

9

Ward III

No matter how hard I try, I always return to the past. How can I not? To start, I've had the book, *Matinee Tomorrow*, dedicated to me from my father: "To Ward III, aged four, who will know the theatre of the next half century. I hope that it will be as exciting for him as it has been for me." I have a treasure trove of letters in leather covered cigar boxes that my father wrote to my mother, with memories of the Broadway theater from my childhood. My father and I went to plays often. He would scribble notes about the plays on a pad. I had a pad, too, and scribbled on it.

We also went to the circus often. The circus in those days was at Madison Square Garden on 50th Street and Eighth Avenue. We went to the side shows down below, where the elephants, the clowns, and the lions in their cages were before they came up to the main auditorium. Once, my father asked me to get up on an elephant with Lee Remick. Using a ladder she climbed up immediately. She was sixteen and I was some ten years younger. She was a cute girl, even at sixteen, and I was a bit in awe of her. Her mother and my father were great friends, and her family was extremely wealthy. Anyway, Lee jumped up on the elephant's back in a heartbeat, and I refused to do it. I never saw her after our circus outing although her mother, Pat Packard, gave me a lot of books when she moved from her floor-through Park Avenue apartment to a smaller place.

My father introduced me to a life that I loved, theater and hotel living—and my mother expanded my introduction into that world, too, giving me Broadway and Off-Broadway seats. My stepfather, Roderick W. Rahe took me fishing and taught me about more general life skills; he was more about "do the homework." I had fun carrying dirt in the backyard of our home in Darien, Connecticut, up to a lawn that never became too much more than a kind of "Charlie Brown" lawn. It was like Jean Shepherd's father's furnace in *A Christmas Story*. It never worked. Anyway, I did work around the house. Friends of mine, whose families were very wealthy, would invite me to their clubs to play tennis, but I felt like an outsider. Occasionally I would tell them, "I have homework to do," but I'd work around the house all day Saturday, helping to build walls and carrying dirt and raking lawns. My parents couldn't afford to hire somebody, even though I thought that would be the very best idea. I think I have calluses to this day from some of the work I did. I'm grateful, in retrospect, that those chores taught me a work ethic.

My stepfather took us on trips. We would go fishing. He would take me and my brothers up to our small island in the Thousand Islands on the Saint Lawrence River straddling New York State and Canada. I had chores to do up there, too. Every day one of my chores was to bail out the boat. It was a long-bowed mahogany boat which leaked like a sieve and would be filled with about two feet of water every morning. I would desperately try to get my friends from neighboring islands to join the fun, like Tom Sawyer. There was no electricity on the island at that time. I used a cast iron bailing pail. It was backbreaking work. You'd bail out the boat and the very next morning there was water in it all over again. When it rained it was even worse. No wonder I wanted a fiberglass boat. Forget about the mahogany.

I had been in plays in high school and, like my father, wrote plays at the time. I was miserable everywhere in high school except on stage. After all, I was really leading two lives. One was with my father in New York, at The Plaza and going to the theater. Another was leading the life of a typical teenager in Darien, Connecticut. The two lives never met. I had one friend, Coles Phinizy, Jr., whose father worked for *Sports Illustrated* who knew of my New York life. But he was it.

While in high school, I did a play for a vaudeville show about Dracula. I ran away from home just before the play was done, and I was gone for three months. Years later, I was invited to speak to students about writing at a school in Lewisburg, West Virginia, by a woman who I had a crush on in high school. She was surprised to hear I had run away. "I didn't know anything about that!" So much for trying to impress her.

I didn't fully realize the grief I would cause my mother and stepfather, being on the road for three months. But I would make it up to them later; in the next more than thirty years, I was not only a dutiful son but a very supportive one. Prayer, which had become second nature to me, was one means of supporting them, as odd as this may sound to some. I had run away from home, yearning to be loved. I didn't find love, but I had the first inkling I wanted to be a writer.

I hitchhiked to Mobile, Alabama. Fifty miles north of Mobile, I almost stripped the gears of the car belonging to one driver. "I thought you could drive," he yelled. But the only driving experience I had really had was running my family's Pontiac into a washing machine in the garage.

Film star Miriam Hopkins in the 1930s. Also from Georgia,
she and my father were great friends. (Ward Morehouse collection)

Somewhere further south another car screeched to a stop. "Get in! I'm happy to see you. Praise the Lord! Here's a check for five dollars," said a cherubic, Bible-quoting, "born again" Christian who seemed like he walked out of the late Albert Maysles' classic documentary about door-to-door Bible salesmen in the 1950s. The check turned out to be good when I cashed it at a Mobile department store, and I got a room for a night and ate nicely for two days.

In Mobile, I got a job with Procter and Gamble. A small group of misfits, including myself, carried big boxes of "samples" strapped around our necks and occasionally dumped remaining samples of detergent on porches of the Negro shanty towns when we were exhausted. In Mobile, my first accommodation was a janitor's broom closet. But after getting the "sample" salesman job, I moved up in the world to a room in the same WMCA.

❀

In high school I was in *The Matchmaker*, Thornton Wilder's play, and starred in Darien community theater productions for two summers. At Franklin College in Indiana I had the lead in *A Doll's House*.

After Franklin, I earnestly studied acting at the American Academy of Dramatic Arts, leaving the Academy before the second year ended to be an apprentice at the American Shakespeare Festival in Stratford, Connecticut. While in Stratford, I started writing plays in earnest. I lived at The Lambs Club in Manhattan and wrote there at night, traveling back to Stratford for shows. My career as a Shakespearean actor almost ended prematurely when, as one of Julius Caesar's royal guards, I came on stage barefoot. The stage manager greeted me with, "What the hell is the matter with you—where are your sandals?!" "They hurt," I murmured. I already had begun to think of myself more as a writer. That's before I read Hemingway said: "There's nothing to writing. All you do is sit down at a typewriter and bleed."

In an effort to emulate Eugene O'Neill, some of whose best plays were set on and around the sea, I sailed aboard a tug-boat bound for Savannah and a commercial fishing boat out of Manhattan's old South Street Seaport when it was a thriving, gangling fish market.

The first play I ever got paid for was a play that Audrey Wood, Tennessee Williams' long-time agent, optioned for $500. A playwright friend of mine, Lea Freeman, who became a Hollywood screenwriter and dialogue "doctor," and I wrote a play called *End of the Road*. It was about two hobos who jump into the Hudson River to end it all. Years earlier Lea had written a play, *The Widow in Green*, which was produced at Broadway's Cort Theatre in 1931, and soon after she went to Hollywood.

When I was going to the acting school, the American Academy of Dramatic Arts, we would have readings of plays, including *Hamlet and Richard III*, in my father's apartment. I acted in a reading with Miriam Hopkins, who was one of the leading movie stars of the early 1930s. She and Bette Davis had a huge rivalry. Bette Davis's star continued to rise. Miriam was in many movies including *Design for Living*, but her Hollywood career soon waned. She was in *Look Homeward Angel* on Broadway. When I was reading *Richard III* or *Hamlet*, my father would inevitably ask, "Pour me a drink!" Because I knew how to tear a passage to tatters. But after my father died, any love of acting faded.

After my father died, I lived with my stepmother, Rebecca Morehouse, for six months. She was a top journalist in her own right, writing for *Time Magazine*, the *New York Times Magazine* and eventually for *Playbill*. Then I checked into the Terminal Hotel on Twenty-Third Street near the Hudson River searching for more colorful characters; it seemed to have been around since the days of sailing ships. Here I started reading Norman Vincent Peale's *The Power of Positive Thinking* and soon after walked into a Christian Science church on 43rd Street near Madison Avenue. Christian Science has been a major part of my life ever since.

During that period, I had many menial jobs. But a year later, in 1969, I got a job on the *New York Post* as a copy boy. The late Richard Watts, the drama critic of the *Post* at the time, gave me a recommendation. He and my father had been great friends since the 1920s. I was paid $100 a week. Three weeks later I was promoted to a makeup assistant and my salary jumped to $300 a week working with printers in the composing room of the paper.

I was able to buy a car and actually drove down to the *Post* at 210 South Street when I worked nights my last year there. After three years, I got a "tryout" for a reporter's job, courtesy of the Newspaper Guild. I covered police and general news stories. But I wasn't made a full-fledged reporter, and Warren Hoge, who was the city editor, said, "Ward you need to go out and work for a small paper."

Throughout these years at the *Post*, I lived at the Lambs Club. My father introduced me to the club when we attended matinee performances of Broadway shows. We'd stop for lunch across the street at the Blue Ribbon Restaurant, which was next to the Hudson Theatre. Years later I wrote a book on the Hudson Theatre, *Discovering the Hudson*. The club itself has moved to 3 West 51st Street, but the gorgeous Sanford White building is still there, now a posh hotel. I paid $20 a week for my room. There were a lot of old actors living there and some had toured the country, back when touring companies crisscrossed America. Early in the 20th century, the Lambs was the most famous theatrical club in the world. Another beautiful theatrical club for actors, The Players Club, was famous because it was once the home of actor Edwin Booth, the brother of the infamous John Wilkes Booth who shot President Lincoln.

❦

The first time I walked into the old *New York Post* on West Street in lower Manhattan, I knew that's where I belonged. Pete Hamill hunched over his typewriter, typing his column named simply "Pete Hamill"; cries of "Copy!" and copy boys running out to the "composing room" with it; the clackety clack of the "hot type" linotype machines transforming molten lead into words that filled newspapers. I wasn't a fast enough writer to become a full reporter after my three-month tryout and I was shifted to the nights as a make-up assistant on the "lobster shift," working midnight to 8 a.m.

I soon began to think more seriously of Warren Hoge's advice. Then on the strength of the stories I did on the *Post* during those "trial" months, I was hired by *The Christian Science Monitor* in Boston and my real writing career began. I was first an assistant editor of the American news section and then I was a reporter for the New England section, a special section within the *Monitor,* which competed with the *Boston Herald* and the *Boston Globe.* I got a lot of scoops. I learned some of the basics from a cyclonic editor who used to yell at me periodically. His name was Leon Lindsay. He would invariably yell his head off if I worked for another section. I tried to explain to him that I worked on the other sections on weekends. The yelling continued, but he was the very first person I had lunch with when I visited the newsroom years later.

I was driven. I would be there at night, I would be there in the morning, out-producing many of the people on the paper. I was absolutely driven to make it back to New York and show the *Post* that I was a good reporter. After four years in Boston, I moved back to New York where I spent six years as a staff correspondent for the *Monitor*. And in 1994 I was hired as a Broadway columnist for the *Post*. I became a sort of star of the *Post* for the next five years. I would not only do the Broadway column for Friday, but on the weekends I would switch over to doing the celebrity stories. One of the reasons I did this is that I had a young child at home. I was paid by the story. I was actually a contributor, even though I made close to $80,000 a year. The column I wrote for the *Post* was called "On and Off-Broadway." After my editor, Matt Diebel, left the paper, my days were numbered. We had a great relationship. It was like my relationship with people on the *Monitor*. I could do no wrong. But once he left, I was out. Actually, leaving the *Post* was one of the best things that ever happened to me because I was able to write books like The Plaza book, *Inside The Plaza*. And also I began to reassess what direction I was going in, in journalism. I'd gone from a very respectable paper like the *Monitor*, which prided itself on accuracy and fairness, to becoming more and more of a Walter Winchell kind of columnist at the *Post*. My father and Winchell were great friends and he respected my father. Winchell respected him as a critic and author. But Winchell, as we saw in the movie *Sweet Smell of Success*, with Burt Lancaster, wasn't always a happy man.

❧

My father was a master of the newspaper interview, probably more than anyone else in the 20th century. He wasn't as literary as, say, Brooks Atkinson. He didn't have the background that Atkinson had. Or Walter Kerr. Kerr's writing didn't flow smoothly sometimes, and he and Atkinson could go off on a tangent and be obtuse. My father was never like that. He was always clear and sometimes even lyrical. So, in my view, he was the best drama critic of the 20th century. Ervin Drake, who died in his 90s and wrote the lyrics to the huge hit *It Was a Very Good Year*, was always extremely complimentary about my father because he had said Drake was in a class with Oscar Hammerstein. People from Helen Hayes, to Katharine Cornell, to the Lunts loved him. One of my father's greatest gifts was remembering a performance that everybody else had forgotten. He had a photographic memory about performances and dates and times, and he could recite the batting average for a lot of the Yankees ball players. He used to be on the phone for hours with Johnny Briscoe, a retired agent living in the Royalton Hotel, and they would be talking dates plays opened, who was in them, and how many performances they ran. Talking by the hour. About Ellen Terry and Maude Adams and James O'Neill, father of Eugene O'Neill ...

Moving On

A month after I lost my job as a Broadway columnist on the *Post*, I became a freelance reporter for the news section, specializing in celebrity reporting. I worked for the city editor, Stuart Marques, who went on to the *New York Daily News*. He liked me because I had worked for him on weekends and got the stories others couldn't. "Don't do too much," Marques counseled me. But I couldn't help myself.

When I worked for the *Post* I sometimes had to write my story standing up. I had a word processor—not a computer of today—and I had to stand up because if I sat down, I'd fall asleep. I had a small office for several years above Broadway's Helen Hayes Theatre.

After leaving the *Post*, I was a columnist on *The New York Sun, AMNewYork*, and *The Epoch Times*. After the *Post*, I never said negative things about an actor or repeated the juiciest gossip about some production. I had changed—not that I had an epiphany but I realized negativity was a dead end.

I was also a columnist on the *Savannah Morning News* at one time. My column was "Manhattan Musings." I did that for a year to earn extra money. It gave me a sense of freedom I didn't have on *The Christian Science Monitor*, which I was working for at the time, because I could write about Central Park or a play I saw. I sort of copied the style of Pete Hamill or Jimmy Breslin and it was a lot of fun to write. I got paid very modestly, $25 per column every week, which in the late '70s was added income. I tried to keep it interesting. They tried to steer me towards people who had some Savannah connection. I interviewed Stacy Keach once. He was from Savannah originally; he was born there. It was fun. It was probably the first inkling I had of doing more personal feature writing which eventually led me to write books.

❧

I got back to writing plays when I was on the *Monitor*. I based some of the characters in my play, *The Actors*, on fellow residents from my days living at the Lambs Club. *The Actors* was about the denizens of a theater club in Times Square living out the remainder of their lives in colorful dreams of the past. Frank Rich reviewed the play in 1982. It was remounted in 1986 and got a lot of nice reviews. The plot was about a club that is going bankrupt, the older actors produce a play to get it out of bankruptcy, and a critic and his son are reunited. Eventually money comes in to pay the mortgage. Members of the Lambs Club came to see it and largely loved it.

Trunk Full of Memories was done in several Off-Broadway venues, as well as Savannah, Georgia, and then remounted as a reading at the 7 Stages Theatre in Atlanta. It's about a family that lives in Savannah, Georgia. My stepmother Rebecca had lost a brother in a car accident so I used that as part of the plot. For years her brother's room was kept exactly the way it was the night he died.

I got a grant for $10,000 in 1987 to mount my play, *My Four Mothers,* at the Jan Hus Theatre—the Jan Hus Church; they have a theater downstairs. It was about a fellow who had

The Joan M., a long-bowed mahogany boat later renamed Showgirl. My mother, Joan Marlowe, is at the wheel. My father, who seldom was seen wearing anything other than a blue suit, sits in back.

four mothers, loosely based upon Jean, Rebecca, my mother, and we had a younger mother in there to make it a little more exciting. The father had died and they're all, not vying for the estate, but crazy about the son. The first reading of it was done at the Lambs Club, and it was like sort of a Neil Simon comedy. *The New York Times* actually gave a good mention to *My Four Mothers* in one of its columns, when the *New York Times* had a weekly theater news column. But the play then became darker and not funny anymore. So I brought in a collaborator, Joseph Koster, and it was then done for several weeks at the Amateur Comedy Club on Sniffen Court on East 36th Street. It was a big hit there. It had a big audience. And it was called *Mother's Day,* changed from *My Four Mothers.*

In 1991 I did a play called *Mr. Doom* at the Kaufman Theater based on my father's play, *Mr. Doom Gets a Letter.* Jean Dalrymple and I spent weeks rewriting my father's original play which had been optioned for Broadway by Morton Gottlieb in the 1960's, when it was offered to Alfred Lunt and Lynn Fontanne. It was about a postman who gets a letter from a former lover and suddenly she shows up at his post office. My father, a friend of the Lunts for decades, hoped they would do the play. But by then they had basically retired from acting.

There were a couple of productions of *Broadway After Dark,* a one-man show I wrote. It was done at the American Theater of Actors and then we took it to the Rainbow Theater in Norwalk, Connecticut, where it got a review from the *New York Times* in 1999. Shortly after that Stewart Lane and I co-wrote a play called *If It Was Easy.* I quoted him continually when on the *Post.* He was a great news source. I had co-written four consecutive stories for the front page of the *New York Post* about Frank Sinatra just after he died. And I called up Stewart, "Do you think you might ever produce a musical about Sinatra?" "Oh, yeah. That sounds like a good idea." So I originated the idea and, of course, the musical has never been done. But the play about producing a Sinatra play got a lot of publicity, and for a change Stewart had people contacting him wanting to invest. We worked on *If It Was Easy* in Connecticut first. He and his wife, actress Bonnie Comeley had rented a home on the Connecticut shore, not far from Westport, and we roughed out some dialogue there and then worked on it at his apartment in New York. The musical about Sinatra never materialized, but our comedic play was about a producer doing a Sinatra musical. Eventually it was done as a reading in a small theater at the Berkshire Playhouse. Then we did it in the summer of 2000 at 7 Stages Theater in Atlanta as a full production with Kevin Dobson who is a well-known TV actor. The American Theatre Critics Association nominated it for Best New Play of the Year. It came to New York a year later—shortly before 9/11—and ran about three months at the Douglas Fairbanks Theatre. While we got a couple of good reviews from smaller newspapers, the major papers weren't so kind. I believe one of the reasons it was attacked was because I had been a columnist on the *Post* and Stewart was a Broadway producer. Stewart and a screenwriter tried to turn it into a screenplay. I then co-wrote a play called *Gangplank*. Set on Lake Ontario, it is about a man who runs a kind of Rick's Café (as in *Casablanca*) on a boat. All of a sudden his long-lost love comes along. She's a Russian who married well but harbors their long-lost love, also. All the characters were mine and my colleague filled out the dialogue. It was done at the American Theatre of Actors. James Jennings gave us his Chernuchin Theatre there in the spring of 2010. It had a nice two-week run. We got a few column mentions but no critics came.

11

Summing Up

Becky and Jean were both mentors. My mother was also a mentor in the sense she was a cheerleader, as she also was for others over the years. She would keep clippings of my articles and was very proud of me. Becky and Jean were the same way. Never critical, really. I think Jean was critical at one point —the time I asked her to pay for the reading of a play, she refused, and I threatened to jump off the Brooklyn Bridge. "That is stupid!" she shot back. But she generously came up with the check and sent it to them. I have a letter I cherish to this day that Jean wrote to my mother. It says, "How proud I am of Ward, the third. Every time I see him I think of his father and how proud he would be of him on *The Christian Science Monitor*." And Becky was the same way. There was a little more friction with Becky because I was competitive with my father. But as I began to appreciate myself more, and my own uniqueness, I had more appreciation for his unique and great contribution to the American theater.

Years later, I used the name of my father's column, "Broadway After Dark," for my own column in the resurrected *New York Sun*, then *AMNewYork*, and now for a website called BroadwayAfterDark.org.

On the *Post* as a Broadway columnist, I had my share of

wrong calls. Such was the media frenzy after Princess Diana died that it seemed almost certain a musical about her life and death would eventually come to Broadway. But my prediction never came true. An Off-Broadway play was done about

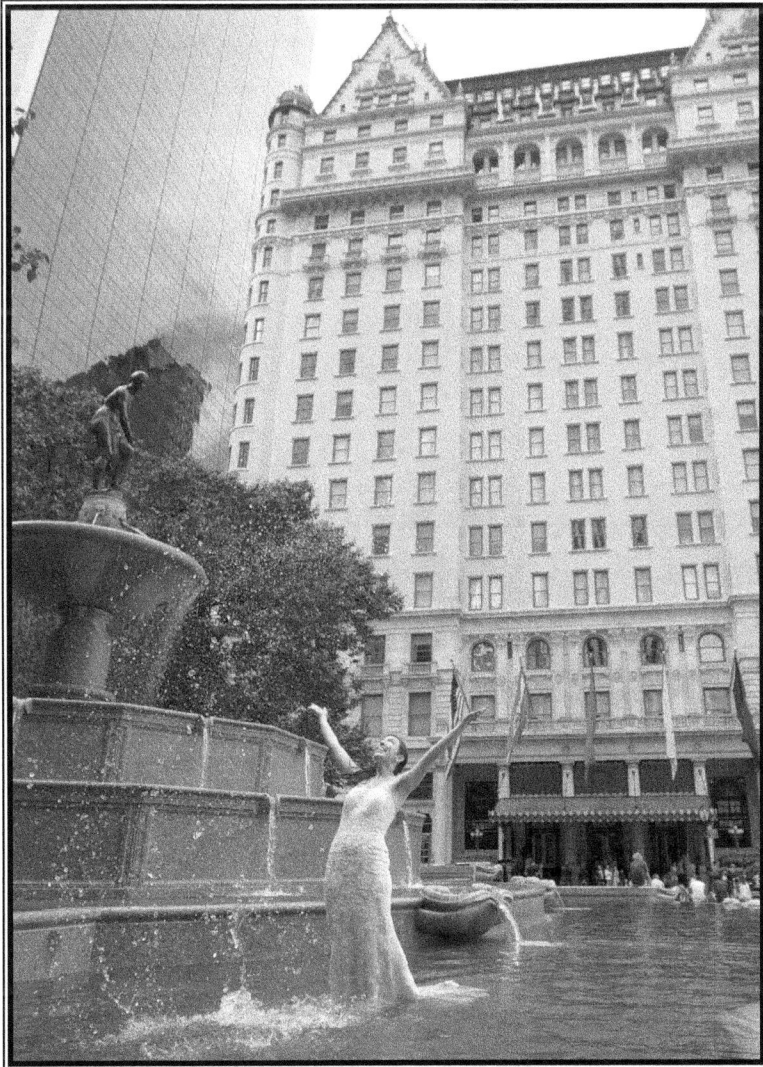

Katherine Boynton cools off in The Plaza's Pulitzer Fountain after our wedding. PHOTO BY BROOK CHRISTOPHER

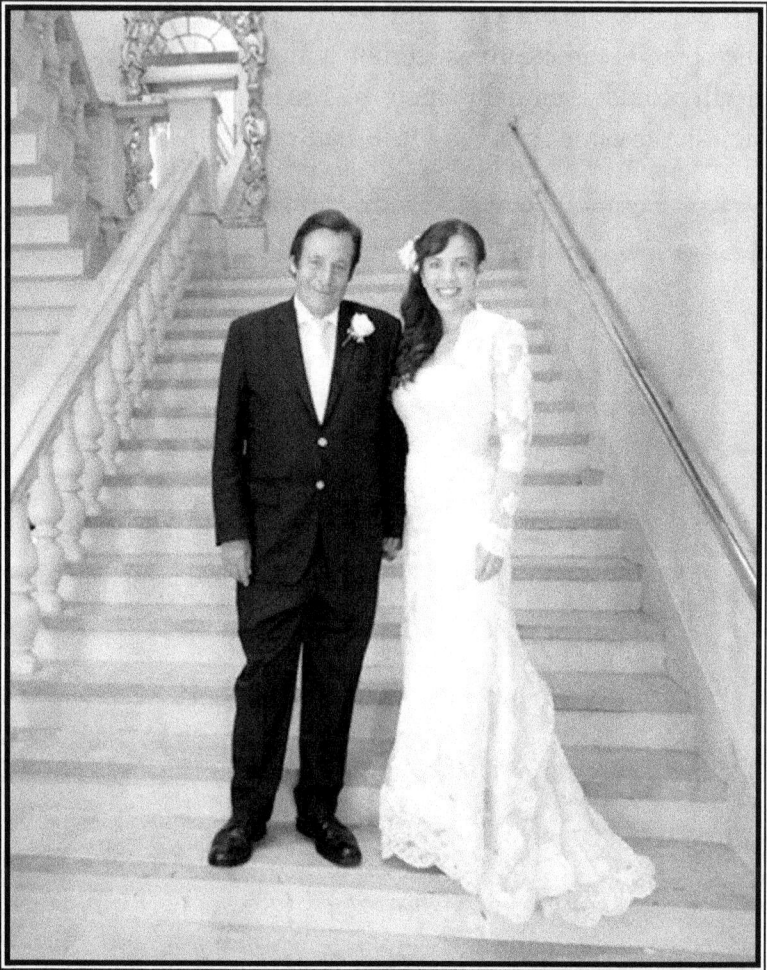

Katherine Boynton and Ward Morehouse III at The Plaza before their wedding brunch. PHOTO BY BROOK CHRISTOPHER

her, however. I was accurate saying a stage version of Disney's megahit movie, *The Lion King*, would come to Broadway. The *New York Times*, in an interview with a Disney executive, confirmed my prediction. I said Whoopi Goldberg would take over for Nathan Lane starring in *A Funny Thing Happened on the Way to the Forum*. She did. When on the *Sun*, I was first with the story that a stage version of *Dirty Rotten Scoundrels* would be on Broadway. But after leaving the *Post* I tired of breaking news stories. I turned more whole-heartedly to writing books, including the one about Broadway's historic Hudson Theatre on West 44th Street which showcased the grit and glamour of a bygone era.

Things came pretty much full circle for me when I married actress Katherine Boynton, who was in a play I reviewed favorably. We were married in the Conservatory Garden in Central Park and our reception was at The Plaza Hotel. My son, Will, was my best man. Unlike Ernest Hemingway's quote about F. Scott Fitzgerald and The Plaza that when Fitzgerald died he should leave his heart to The Plaza, I didn't have to die to leave my heart to The Plaza. It has, after all, played a significant role in my life—and for a period of time, in that of a bear who lived at The Plaza.

LONDON'S GREATEST GRAND HOTELS
by Ward Morehouse III and Katherine Boynton,
a sequel to Ward Morehouse III's *London's Grand Hotels*
published by BearManor Media in 2010.

"In LONDON'S GRAND HOTELS, Ward Morehouse III bangs his fist down imperiously on the bell desk, shouts 'Front, please!' and commands to appear, one after another, London's most celebrated hostelries. Each, as it were, disrobes—revealing for readers the inspired tricks of luxury and hospitality that have kept generations of happy customers coming back. If you cannot stay anytime soon at the Savoy, the May Fair, the Connaught, the Stafford, the Ritz or their like, then do the next best thing and enjoy them vicariously through Mr. Morehouse's delightful book."
—*Alan Farnham, Contributing Editor, Forbes*

LONDON'S GRAND HOTELS: *Extraordinary People, Extraordinary Service in the World's Cultural Capital,*
By Ward Morehouse III
published by BearManor Media in 2010

Ward Morehouse III's love affair with grand hotels began long before he wrote his first landmark book, *THE WALDORF-ASTORIA: America's Gilded Dream*, which was followed by *INSIDE THE PLAZA: An Ultimate Portrait of the Ultimate Hotel.*

His father, the late drama critic Ward Morehouse (who requested "Room Service, please!" on his tombstone), lovingly indoctrinated his young son into the glamorous life of luxurious hotels in New York, London and elsewhere, teaching him that a great hotel is made up of more than fine linens and fancy uniforms—that it is the staff, the people, who make any hotel special.

LONDON'S GRAND HOTELS: Extraordinary People, Extraordinary Service in the World's Cultural Capital, published by BearManor Media in 2010, is a captivating look beyond the physical grandeur of London's top hotels to the grand people working in—and staying at—these real-life palaces. London boasts the greatest collection of grand hotels of any city, and, says Morehouse, checking into any one of them is like taking part in a grand opera. His book abounds with colorful anecdotes and delightful behind-the-scenes stories of the hotels, their owners, their staff, and their famous guests—which include some of the world's leading writers, filmmakers, politicians and stars.

In *LONDON'S GRAND HOTELS*, he presents twenty-seven of London's luxury hotels, beginning with Brown's, established in 1837, and including Claridge's; Bailey's; The Savoy, The Ritz; and The May Fair, to more recently established hotels such as The Halkin; Soho Hotel, The Metropolitan, and Haymarket Hotel. Through their doors and onto the pages walk such illustrious guests as Rudyard Kipling, Theodore Roosevelt, F. Scott Fitzgerald; Winston Churchill; Queen Elizabeth, Laurence Olivier, Charlie Chaplin; Cary Grant, Katharine Hepburn; Humphrey Bogart; Lauren Bacall; Woody Allen, Elizabeth Taylor, Richard Burton, and many, many more. The book also contains exclusive celebrity photographs of current theater, film and business stars who are devotees of hotels discussed—such as Meryl Streep; Hugh Grant; Jude Law, Sir Ian McKellen and Sir Richard Branson.

"England's legendary empire truly lives on through its greatest inns," says Morehouse. In *LONDON'S GRAND HOTELS* he guides us on a mesmerizing, magical "inside tour" to some of its very best. It is a book to be savored by the armchair traveler, those who love behind-the-scenes celebrity stories, and anyone fascinated with the charm and history of the places they have visited—or hope to visit in the future.

ABOUT THE AUTHOR: Ward Morehouse III is the author of three previous books on hotels: *THE WALDORF-ASTORIA: America's Gilded Dream; INSIDE THE PLAZA: An Intimate Portrait of the Ultimate Hotel; and LIFE AT THE TOP: Inside New York's Grand Hotels*. He has also written a book about New York's historic Hudson Theatre *(DISCOVERING THE HUDSON: New York's Landmark Theater from Broadway's Beginnings to Live Television, Jack Paar and Elvis)* as well as *BROADWAY AFTER DARK*, which contains columns celebrating Broadway written by him and by his father, the late Ward Morehouse, a well-known drama critic and columnist. It was his father who introduced him to the luxurious hotel life. His books combine that fascination with his passion for the theater. Ward Morehouse III was chief theater columnist for the *New York Post* from 1994 to 1998 and continues to contribute to its news and celebrity pages today. He also has written theater pieces for the *Christian Science Monitor,* Reuters News Service, *People.com,* and *Inside.com.* He is Editor of the popular *BroadwayAfterDark.org* website and wrote the monthly Checking In column for *Travel Smart Newsletter*, which *Money Magazine* called the "Best Newsletter for Travelers on a Budget." In addition, he is the author of the off-Broadway plays "The Actors," "If It Was Easy" (co-written with Stewart F. Lane), "Gangplank," and "Beloved Broadway" and he wrote the book for the musical, "A Night at the Astor" (music by David Romeo). He resides in New York City.

CONTACT: KAY RADTKE, 212-535-6009, E-MAIL: KYRADTKE@AOL.COM

LONDON'S GRAND HOTELS: Extraordinary People, Extraordinary Service in the World's Cultural Capital, by Ward Morehouse III • Publication Date: November 1, 2010 • Paperback: $21.95 • ISBN: 1 59393 117 4 • Photographs • Index
Visit www.londonsgrandhotels.com

PREVIOUS BOOKS BY WARD MOREHOUSE III

THE WALDORF-ASTORIA:
America's Gilded Dream
(M. Evans & Co.)

"The grand cities of the world have their grand hotels, the bed-and-breakfasts for the mighty and moneyed. Ward Morehouse III explores one of New York City's grandest in T*he Waldorf-Astoria: America's Gilded Dream* ...Morehouse writes of pleasures and scandals, of the hard facts of running a hotel and of its romance. The hotel comes off well in the hands of its appreciative Boswell and one will find 'The Waldorf-Astoria' to be a pleasant buffet."
— *The New York Times Book Review*

INSIDE THE PLAZA:
An Intimate Portrait of the Ultimate Hotel
(Applause Theatre & Cinema Books)

"What do Ward Morehouse III and Kay Thompson's Eloise have in common? The theater critic, playwright and author of a previous hotel biography (The Waldorf-Astoria: America's Gilded Dream) and the six-year-old scamp both did some growing up at New York's fabled Plaza Hotel. In

Inside The Plaza: An Intimate Portrait of the Ultimate Hotel, Morehouse details its sparkling history, from the architectural (the hotel's gables and balconies were fashioned by hand) to the social (at the masked ball Truman Capote threw for Katherine Graham, Candice Bergen wore a mask topped with bunny ears). Toss in stories (and black-and-white photographs) of nightclub chanteuses, rock stars and American royalty, as well as tidbits about underground railroad tracks for transporting coal and Prohibition-era liquor sales, and it's an entertaining read for travelers and homebodies alike."

—Publishers Weekly

LIFE AT THE TOP:
Inside New York's Grand Hotels
(BearManor)

"There is no one more qualified to write about New York's grand hotels than Ward Morehouse III, having been reared in two of the grandest whose histories he would later write. An eminent theater columnist and feature reporter, Morehouse is able to bring the Big Apple's glamorous (or once glamorous) hostelries to life, mixing history with delicious gossip and amusing anecdotes that only an insider would be privy to. Luxury hotels provide a heightened sense of life and fun for the rich and famous as well as the ordinary guest, and Morehouse catches the excitement of the hotel as playground perfectly."
    —Frederick M. Winship, Critic-at-Large, United Press International

"Ward Morehouse III's fabulous take on New York's greatest hotels reads like the legendary stories of Damon Runyon. He breathes new life into these wonderful old metropolitan inns and the colorful characters that inhabited them."

—Bill Hoffmann, New York Post

Also by Ward Morehouse:

DISCOVERING THE HUDSON: New York's Landmark Theater from Broadway's Beginnings to Live Television, Jack Parr and Elvis (BearManor)

BROADWAY AFTER DARK (BearManor)

www.ingramcontent.com/pod-product-compliance
Lightning Source LLC
LaVergne TN
LVHW021544080426
835509LV00019B/2826